NATURE DETECTIVE

Birds

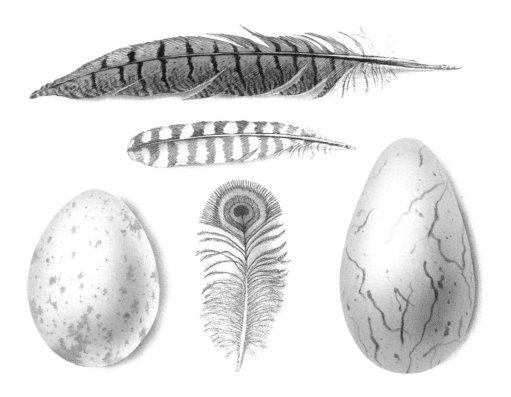

ANITA GANERI

Illustrated by Danny Flynn

FRANKLIN WATTS
NEW YORK · LONDON · TORONTO · SYDNEY

© 1992 Franklin Watts

Published in the United States
in 1992 by
Franklin Watts, Inc.

Ganeri, Anita, 1961–
    Birds / Anita Ganeri.
      p.   cm. — (Nature detective)
    Includes index.
    Summary: Describes the characteristics and life cycle of a variety
of birds, provides birdwatching tips, and features instructions for
making of bird bath, bird sketches, and other projects.
    ISBN 0-531-14180-2
    1. Birds—Miscellanea—Juvenile literature. 2. Birds—
Identification—Juvenile literature. [1. Birds.] I. Title.
II. Series: Nature detective (New York, N.Y.)
QL676.2.G36 1992b   91–39790
598—dc20   CIP AC

Designer: Splash Studio
Editor: Sarah Ridley
Additional Illustrations: Terry Pastor

Printed in Belgium.

Contents

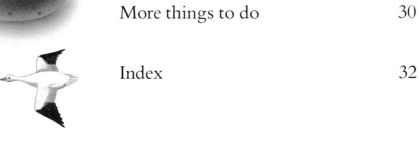

What is a bird?

The first known bird, *Archaeopteryx*, lived about 150 million years ago at the time of the dinosaurs. We know what it looked like because of fossils found in the last century. It was the first creature to have feathers, but it also had claws and a bony tail, like its reptile ancestors. Today there are over 9,200 species of living birds. They are divided into 27 orders, or groups. The largest order is the perching birds, which makes up over half of all living birds. The song thrush shown here is a member of this group.

Birds are warm-blooded, air-breathing vertebrates (animals with backbones). They all lay eggs, and many build nests in which to raise their young. All birds have wings and feathers, even if they no longer have the ability to fly. Flying birds all share the same streamlined body shape, perfectly designed for flight. Flightless birds, on the other hand, have developed different parts of their bodies to help them survive.

In many places, you will see birds simply by looking up into the sky. However, to learn more about the lives of the fascinating variety of birds, there are many clues and signs to look out for around you. The size and color of a bird's features will help you to identify what species of bird it is.

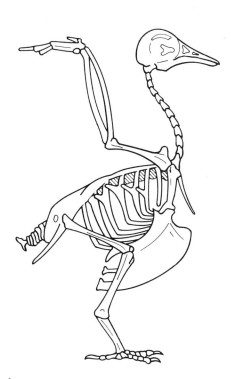

Skeleton
A bird needs to be as light as possible to fly well. Flying birds have hollow bones, resulting in very light skeletons.

Feathers Birds are the only animals with feathers. These are used for flight, insulation, waterproofing, and streamlining. Their color helps birds identify each other and is also used in camouflage, courtship, and threatening behavior.

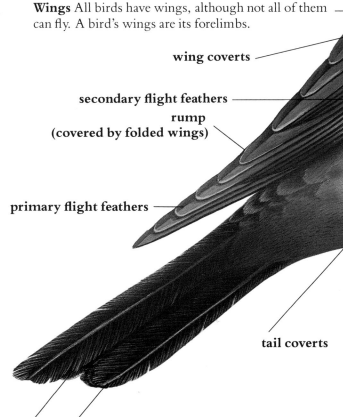

Wings All birds have wings, although not all of them can fly. A bird's wings are its forelimbs.

wing coverts

secondary flight feathers

rump
(covered by folded wings)

primary flight feathers

tail coverts

Tail A bird's tail is made up of feathers. It is not a true tail, like that of a cat, as it does not have bones down the middle. Birds use their tails for balance, steering, lift-off, braking, courtship, and threatening displays.

nape

ear (hidden by feathers)

Eyes Eyesight is the most important sense for many birds. It is vital for navigation in the air. Birds have large eyes compared to their size. They also have mobile necks so that they can look around them. By contrast, some birds, such as oilbirds, can locate and catch their prey in darkness, using only their ears.

nostril

Beak Birds do not have heavy jaws or teeth. Instead, they have strong but light beaks for feeding, preening, and occasionally courtship.

Breast The breastbone is a huge, broad bone for anchoring the wing muscles.

flank

ankle

Leg A bird's knee looks as if it is pointing back to front. In fact, this is the bird's ankle. Its knee is farther up its leg, covered by feathers.

toe

Feet Most birds have three or four toes. Perching birds, including the song thrush, have three toes pointing forwards and one pointing backwards, for gripping on to branches.

Where do birds live?

Birds are found all over the world, from the freezing Arctic and Antarctic to the tropical rainforests, and from remote islands to people's backyards. Birds are so widespread because, like mammals, they are warm-blooded. Their body temperature remains constant under most weather conditions. This means that they can stay active even when it is very hot or very cold. The power of flight has also given many birds the ability to travel and make use of food sources beyond the reach of other animals.

Wherever they are found, birds have adapted to suit their surroundings. Their appearance and behavior are linked to their habitat. When you spot a bird, try to discover how it has adapted to where it lives.

Seashore birds

These are some of the birds you might see feeding along the seashore, nesting on cliffs, or soaring over the sea on the lookout for food.

1 Dunlin Large flocks of dunlins feed in estuaries and along coasts. They belong to the group of birds known as waders. They have long bills for probing the seashore in search of snails, worms, crabs, and other creatures.

2 Herring gull Gulls glide over the sea on the lookout for prey. Some gulls smash small shellfish open by carrying them up in the air, and then dropping them on the rocks below.

3 Eider duck This sea duck breeds on rocky coasts and islands. It builds its nest from seaweed and grass, lined with downy feathers.

4 Oystercatcher   5 Gulls   6 Terns

Woodland birds

A great variety of birds live in woodlands and forests all over the world. They can be found high up in the tree tops, on tree trunks, and on the ground.

1 Woodpecker Many woodpeckers use their strong, pointed beaks to chisel into tree trunks to reach insect grubs under the bark. They have long sticky or barbed tongues for pulling the grubs out.

2 Long-eared owl This owl roosts on tree trunks and branches during the day. The ground around the roost may be littered with pellets containing the remains of the owl's prey (see page 19). Other species of owl roost in barns or in holes in trees.

3 Pheasant These birds live on the forest floor. They have short legs, rounded wings and long, pointed tails. They are fast runners but reluctant fliers.

4 Treecreeper   5 Thrush

AMAZING FACTS

Six species of penguin, including the emperor penguin, live and breed on the freezing icy wastes of Antarctica. There are no penguins in the Northern Hemisphere, at the other end of the world.

Almost half of all the world's species of birds live in the South American rainforests. They include toucans, parrots, and hummingbirds.

Sandgrouse live in hot, dry deserts. The parent birds fly up to 50 miles a day to get water for their chicks. They soak their breast feathers with water, at a waterhole, and then fly back to the chicks who drink the tiny droplets clinging to their feathers.

Lake and river birds

Many birds live on or near fresh water, in ponds, lakes, rivers, and canals. A lot of water birds are strong swimmers. Others keep watch for food from the water's edge, or from tree branches.

1 Kingfisher The kingfisher hovers or perches above the river and dives in after its prey. It can also brake in midair to dive for fish. It builds its nest in a tunnel in the river bank.

2 Mute swan The mute swan is found on lakes, rivers, and canals. Swans walk clumsily on land but are powerful swimmers. They build their nests of waterweeds and reeds close to the water.

3 Heron The heron stands quite still in the water, waiting for fish to swim by. Then it stabs the fish with its long, pointed beak. Herons are some of the biggest river birds.

4 Mallard   5 Moorhen   6 Canada geese

Town and city birds

Even if you live in a busy town or city, you will still be able to see many types of birds. Some of these have adapted to city life because their wild habitats have been destroyed. Others take advantage of the warmth, safety, and food available in towns.

Bird-watching

Wherever you go to watch birds, remember not to frighten or disturb them. Use the cover of hedges and bushes to hide yourself, and avoid wearing brightly colored clothes.

You will see a lot of birds just by walking outside, but the countryside is home to many more different species of birds. As you become more serious about bird-watching, the following items may help.

A field guide For identifying any birds you might see and not recognize at once.

A notebook and pencils When you see a bird, note down what it looks like, or draw a quick sketch. You should also keep notes of where and when you saw the bird and what it was doing.

Binoculars Choose a light pair of binoculars that you feel comfortable with. Binoculars graded 7 x 35 (7=magnification; 35=diameter of lens) are good for general bird-watching. These can be expensive, however.

A magnifying glass, a pair of plastic tweezers, and **plastic bags** are good for examining and collecting feathers, pellets, and food remains.

Camera A 35-mm single-lens reflex (SLR) camera is good for taking bird pictures. However, cameras are expensive and a notebook can be just as useful for recording the birds you have seen.

1 House martin House martins often build their mud and saliva nests in groups under the eaves of buildings in towns and cities. The nest is almost completely enclosed which sets it apart from the swallow's nest, with its open bowl shape.

2 Domestic pigeon Pigeons are a common sight in many towns, especially in parks. They also stroll along the streets in search of scraps of food. Their nests are often built on the ledges of city buildings.

3 House sparrow

Why do birds have feathers?

Feathers are what separate birds from the rest of the animal kingdom. They help birds to fly. Among other advantages, this allows birds to escape their enemies successfully. All birds have feathers, although some have more than others. Swans have over 25,000 feathers, compared with less than a thousand on a hummingbird.

Apart from helping birds to fly, feathers have several other uses. They keep birds warm and waterproof. Their colors are used to send signals to other birds and are useful as camouflage. The feathers on the different parts of a bird's body vary in shape, size, and in the job they do.

Tail feathers Quite long, stiff feathers. They come in a great range of sizes, colors, and shapes. They are used for steering in the air, balancing in the air and on the ground, braking, and in courtship or threatening displays.

Wing feathers Long, strong feathers. These are essential for flying. They provide a smooth surface for air to flow over and help to lift the bird up in the air.

Down feathers Short, fluffy feathers next to the bird's skin. They trap air and so help to keep the bird warm. They are also used to line nests.

Body or contour feathers These are often quite short, with a downy base. They give the bird's body its shape. They are also used in camouflage and courtship displays.

What are feathers?

Feathers are made from a protein called keratin. This is the same substance that makes up nails, horns, and reptiles' scales. It gives feathers their great strength and flexibility.

Birds take great care of their feathers. They preen them with their bills to keep them clean and in good condition. They also oil them to keep them waterproof using oil from a gland hidden in feathers above the tail. Once or twice a year, most birds shed their old, worn-out feathers and replace them with new ones. This is called molting.

tip

outer vane

inner vane

barbs

shaft

Thousands of barbules on either side of each barb hook together, like teeth in a zipper, to give the feather a smooth surface.

Looking at feathers

From the size, shape, and color of feathers you find lying on the ground, try to identify the type of bird they belonged to. Which part of the bird's body do the feathers come from? What job did they do? Why are they lying on the ground? Use a field guide to help you check colors and patterns. With practice, you will soon be able to "read" feathers quite easily.

If you are collecting feathers, take them home in a plastic bag to stop them from getting damaged. Use your fingers to preen them gently into shape, then tape them into a scrapbook. Make a note of where you found the feathers and, if you can, which species of bird they belonged to.

How do birds fly?

Birds are not the only animals capable of flight. Insects and bats can fly, too, but not nearly as far or as fast as birds. Birds owe their incredible flying ability to the shape of their wings. These have an airfoil shape, meaning that they are curved on top and flat underneath. As a bird flaps its wings and air passes over them, the airfoil creates a region of low pressure above the wing and high pressure below it. This pushes the wing up and keeps the bird airborne. Aircraft wings use the same design shape.

The power of flight has made birds a highly successful group of animals. It allows them to escape from their enemies, exploit food sources, and migrate to warmer places to breed.

The parts of a buzzard's wing

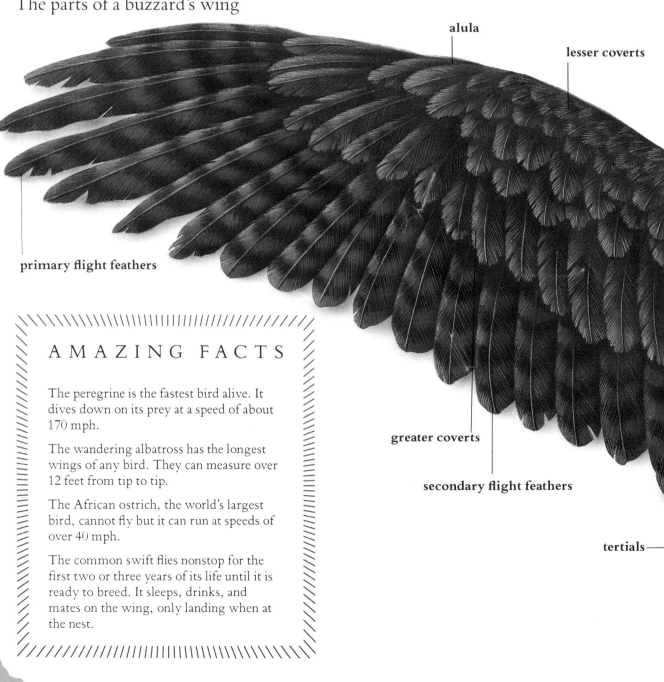

alula

lesser coverts

primary flight feathers

greater coverts

secondary flight feathers

tertials

AMAZING FACTS

The peregrine is the fastest bird alive. It dives down on its prey at a speed of about 170 mph.

The wandering albatross has the longest wings of any bird. They can measure over 12 feet from tip to tip.

The African ostrich, the world's largest bird, cannot fly but it can run at speeds of over 40 mph.

The common swift flies nonstop for the first two or three years of its life until it is ready to breed. It sleeps, drinks, and mates on the wing, only landing when at the nest.

Wing shapes and flight patterns

Various species of bird have different flight patterns which are related to their wing shapes and behavior. Look out for the pattern a bird makes in the air. It will help you decide which species of bird you are looking at. Does it flap its wings or soar? In general, birds with rounded wings tend to fly in short bursts, while pointed wings indicate speed.

Bullfinch Round, broad wings, common to all finches. It flies in short bursts of bouncing flight as it beats its wings, then half closes, and then beats its wings again. It flies like this to save energy.

Canada goose Long, broad wings that help on its long-distance migration. It has a straight flight and constantly beats its wings. It flies with neck outstretched and legs tucked under its body.

Swift Long, curved, slim wings for continuous, rapid flight. Fast beats of the wings are followed by short glides. It swoops to catch insects in midair and spends much of its life airborne.

Herring gull Slim, pointed wings for gliding on the air currents rising over sea cliffs. Apart from gliding, gulls also fly in a straight flight, flapping their wings slowly.

 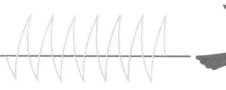 

Kestrel Long, pointed wings. It hovers quite still above the ground in search of prey. To provide lift and stability it beats its wings and fans its tail out. It has a flapping flight.

Why do birds migrate?

Each autumn, many birds leave their summer breeding grounds and set off on journeys, called migrations. They fly to warmer climates where food is more plentiful. In Europe and North America, birds tend to fly south to warmer areas. The next spring, they fly north again to breed.

Birds seem to know instinctively that it is time to migrate. Look out for birds preparing for their flight. They start feeding all the time to build up fat reserves, and they grow increasingly restless. Amazingly, they follow the same route year after year to the same place. We still don't fully understand how birds navigate with such accuracy. Some seem to use the position of the sun or stars in the sky. Others use landmarks, such as mountains and valleys. Some may use the earth's magnetic field to guide them.

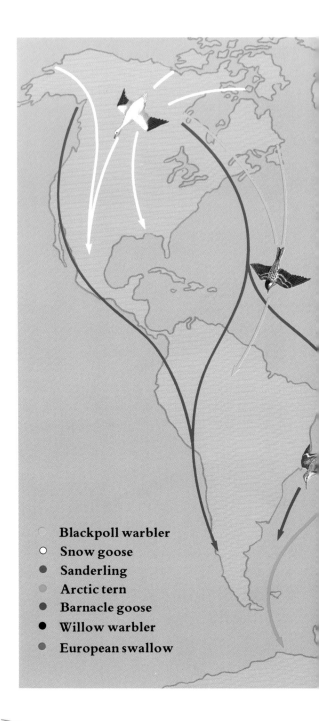

- ○ **Blackpoll warbler**
- ○ **Snow goose**
- ● **Sanderling**
- ● **Arctic tern**
- ● **Barnacle goose**
- ● **Willow warbler**
- ● **European swallow**

Blackpoll warbler This warbler migrates from Canada and the northern states through the eastern United States to South America. Here it will find plentiful supplies of insects to eat.

Snow goose Snow geese breed in the Arctic, then fly south in winter to their feeding grounds in southern parts of the United States. They fly the length of North America on their migration, a distance of about 1,700 miles. Most birds find the way on their first migration by instinct. But snow geese adults lead their young the first time.

Sanderling Sanderlings and other Arctic waders, such as sandpipers, turnstones, and knots, breed in the far north, then migrate south to spend the winter on muddy seashores and estuaries. Sanderlings may migrate down the coast as far south as Chile.

Arctic tern This tern makes the longest migration of any bird. In autumn, it leaves its breeding grounds in the Arctic, northern Europe, and northern Canada to fly south to Antarctica to feed. This makes a one-way trip of over 12,000 miles. Including the return trip, an Arctic tern possibly flies nonstop for about eight months of the year. In this way, it sees more daylight than any other bird while exploiting food sources at both ends of the earth.

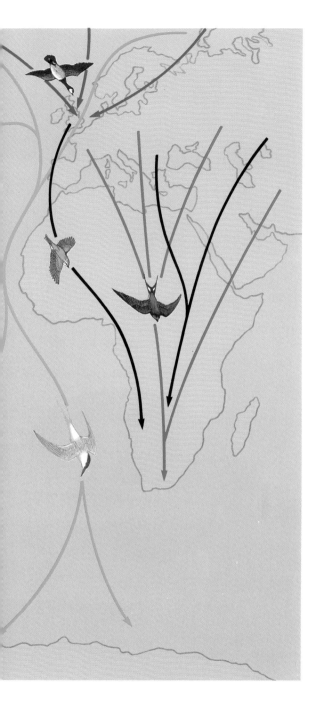

Willow warbler These warblers migrate from Europe to tropical West Africa and some even cross the equator. They make a one-way trip of up to 7,500 miles.

European swallow It leaves Europe in October when its prey of flying insects is scarce, and migrates to South Africa, where food is plentiful. This makes a one-way journey of about 2,500 miles. It returns in March to breed. Bird watchers in Europe look for huge flocks of swallows gathering before they migrate.

Migrating flocks

Many birds migrate in large, noisy flocks. Most fly in a haphazard way, but some follow a set formation. Look out for some of these common flock shapes.

Geese travel in a V-shape, or in a long, wavy line with birds taking turns to lead.

Plovers and other wading birds fly in a large mass, like a shoal of fish. It is difficult to tell which bird is the leader.

Ducks make a slanting line or V-shape as they migrate south.

Barnacle goose The breeding grounds of this goose are in Greenland, Spitzbergen, and NW Arctic Russia. It migrates south to Europe in the autumn to avoid the cold and food shortages of an icy winter. It cruises at about 35 mph, and covers a distance of nearly 780 miles. Most geese stagger their return journey so that they do not arrive before their plant food has grown.

Beaks and bills

Birds do not have teeth, so they use their beaks to catch and hold on to food. The size and shape of a bird's beak will often give a good idea of what that bird eats and how it finds its food. Some beaks also have special features to help a bird tackle a particular type of food. For example, the 13 species of finch on the Galapagos Islands off Ecuador show the close relationship between the type of beak a bird has and what it eats. The finches all look very similar, but each has evolved a different beak to deal with different food.

Although birds mainly use their beaks for feeding, they also play an important part in preening and nest building. Some birds, such as herons, use their beaks in courtship.

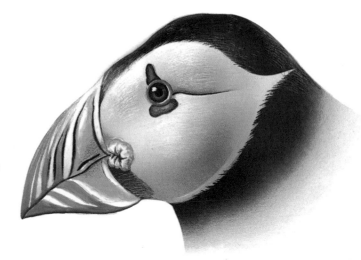

Puffin The puffin has a large beak which is brightly colored in the breeding season (see page 24). There are special spines on its tongue and upper part of the beak to allow the puffin to carry 50 or more sand eels crosswise in its beak. It takes these back to its young in the nesting burrow.

Pigeon Pigeons have strong, blunt-ended beaks for eating seeds. They eat the seeds whole rather than cracking them open as a finch would. They also use their beaks as drinking straws.

Starling The starling's pointed, all-purpose beak is the most common beak shape of all. Look out for these birds picking up seeds and probing your lawn for insect grubs or worms.

Curlew This bird uses its long, curved beak to probe for worms, crustacea, and mollusks buried deep in the seashore mud. Its beak allows it to find food beyond the reach of other shore feeders. Curlews also use their beaks for picking up crabs on the tide line.

Mallard The mallard's beak is broad and flat and is mainly used for a type of feeding called dabbling. This is when the duck skims its beak across the surface of the water, sucking in water and forcing it out again. The beak has fringed edges which sieve plants and seeds from the water. It also feeds by up-ending in the water.

Kestrel The kestrel has a hooked beak, typical of birds of prey. This is used for tearing the meat from mice and other small animals. Kestrels also eat insects and the occasional small bird.

Unusual beaks

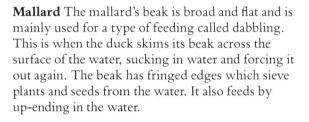

Sword-billed hummingbirds have 4 inch long beaks that are longer than their bodies. They are used for reaching nectar deep inside tropical flowers. The nectar is licked up through long, tubelike tongues inside the bills.

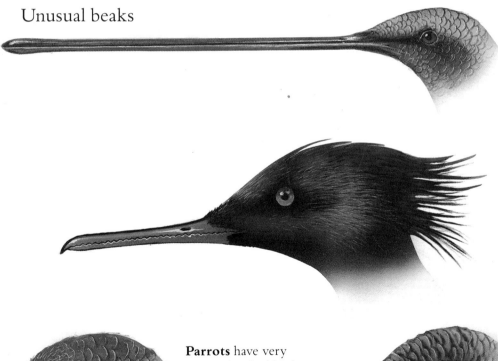

Red-breasted mergansers are sawbill ducks. Their narrow beaks have serrated edges like saw blades. These are used instead of teeth to get a firm grip on fish.

Parrots have very strong, hooked beaks for cracking open seeds and nuts. They use the hooked tip to hold fruit and pull the pulp out. Nuts are cracked in the jaws near the base of the beak.

Crossbills have very specialized, crossed-over beaks for prising seeds out of pinecones. Young crossbills have normal beaks which cross over later.

Who eats what?

Birds need to eat frequently simply to stay alive and to get enough energy for flying, nest building, and breeding. With no teeth to chew their food, birds have developed a very muscular stomach which grinds their food up. Many birds also swallow grit or stones to help this process.

Seeds, fruit, vegetables, worms, nectar, insects, fish, and grass are the most common foods eaten by birds. Most birds find their own food, though some, such as skuas and gulls, are skilled scavengers. They attack other seabirds in midair, forcing them to drop their catch of fish which the scavengers quickly scoop up.

Gannet This bird plunges from heights of 100 feet to catch fish underwater. It folds its wings back as it dives. Air sacs under the skin around its breast act as shock absorbers when the bird hits the water.

Buzzard Soaring in the sky for hours, the buzzard looks out for its food of rabbits, carrion (dead animals), frogs, birds, and field mice. If you find a patch of feathers or fur on the ground, it may indicate that a buzzard hunts in the area.

Oystercatcher During the winter when the oystercatcher is living on the coast, it uses its beak to probe in the mud and on the surface for mussels and other shellfish. It uses the tip of its beak like a hammer to smash shells open or to prise them apart.

House sparrow The sparrow is mainly a seed-eater. It cracks open seeds with its short, tough beak to get to the kernel inside. It also eats nuts, fruit, and insects. In towns it can survive on household snacks.

Magpie A scavenger, the magpie will eat almost anything it can find. This includes insects, worms, plants, seeds, nuts, carrion, berries, small mammals, small birds, their eggs and young, and even leftover food in household garbage.

White-fronted goose
Geese are among the few types of birds that can survive on a diet of grass. They also eat waterplants, grains, clover, and seeds.

Clues from leftovers

Keep a lookout for leftovers, droppings, and other signs of feeding, then try to identify the type of bird that has left them. Here are some examples of the sort of clues you might find.

Many birds leave white or greenish gray droppings. However, the droppings of fruit-eating birds, such as blackbirds, may be colored purple with berry juice and contain seeds.

Look out for some of these leftovers.

In England, pecked or broken snail shells are often left by thrushes. Song thrushes have regular sites called anvils where they smash open snail shells.

Nuts may have rough holes pecked in them. Look out for beak marks on the shells which may have been made by jays or nuthatches.

Pecked apples and pecked corn may be the work of pigeons.

Dropped seeds and berries may indicate that birds have passed overhead or are roosting in trees nearby.

Gulls and crows sometimes leave chipped pieces of eggshell behind after they have raided another bird's nest and eaten the eggs and young.

Tell-tale pellets

When birds swallow their prey, they often take in parts that they cannot digest, such as bones, fur, feathers, shells, and wing cases. So, once or twice a day, owls and many other birds regurgitate these objects in a pellet.

To discover exactly what the bird has been eating, analyze a pellet or two by soaking them in warm water so that you can tease the pellet apart. By doing this you can build up a picture of what the bird eats.

Barn owls produce black or gray, spherical or long and tapered pellets. These contain the bones and fur of rodents, such as moles and mice, that they eat.

Curlews' pellets contain fragments of crab shells and sometimes the hard jaws of the seashore worms that they consume.

curlew pellet

barn owl pellet

19

Night hunters

Very few birds are active at night, and most of these are owls. They take over where the daytime birds of prey, the raptors, leave off. Like falcons and hawks, owls are superb hunters. Their bodies are completely adapted for finding food at night, and it is these adaptations that give the birds their characteristic shape and features.

Nocturnal birds have several advantages over daytime birds. There is less competition for food and they have access to nocturnal prey. They are also safe from daytime predators.

Wings and feathers Powerful wings with soft fringes on the feathers break up the airflow. This allows owls to fly silently and surprise their prey.

fringe

Beak The strong, sharp beak is for tearing meat. It curves downwards so as not to get in the line of sight.

Eyes Owls have superb eyesight. Their huge forward-pointing eyes allow them to judge distances very accurately. The pupils of the eyes enlarge at night to collect as much light as possible. They contract during the day so that the owls are not dazzled.

Facial disks Flat, oval disks of feathers around the eyes. These disks probably help to channel sounds into the ears, as our earflaps do.

Ears Owls' ears give them excellent hearing for locating prey in pitch darkness. The ears are large, vertical slits hidden behind feathers around the eyes. Many owls have one ear higher and bigger than the other for pinpointing prey exactly.

Neck Owls cannot swivel their eyeballs very far but have flexible necks so that they can turn their whole heads around to look and listen behind them.

Talons The sharp, hooked talons on owls' feet are used for grasping, carrying, and tearing prey.

Legs and toes Feathers on their legs and toes muffle the sound for a silent approach. They may also protect owls' legs from being bitten by prey.

The whip-poor-will

Whip-poor-wills feed mainly at dusk, eating moths and other insects which they catch in flight. They have tiny beaks, but can open their mouths very wide to scoop in their prey. Whip-poor-wills have a fringe of fine bristles around their mouths. These may help to direct food into their mouths or to feel for food in the dark. Whip-poor-wills are silent, graceful fliers, like giant moths.

During the day, whip-poor-wills roost on the ground among dead leaves and twigs, or lie along a tree branch. They are perfectly camouflaged by their brown, cream, and black feathers and are almost impossible to spot.

Spotting nocturnal birds

The best time to look for nocturnal birds is at dusk when many of them are setting out to look for food. Look out for their silhouettes as they fly. Many owls have a slow, floating flight. Listen for their distinctive hoots, shrieks, and wailing calls as they stake out their territories.

During the day, look out for pellets lying underneath trees (see page 19). These are signs that an owl has been roosting nearby.

AMAZING FACTS

The nocturnal kakapo from New Zealand is the only parrot that cannot fly. (Male kakapos have very loud mating calls to attract females in the dark.)

Oilbirds live deep inside caves in South America. Inside the caves, they use echolocation to find their way around. They make tiny clicking sounds which hit the cave walls, or other birds, and send back echoes. From these, the oilbirds can tell where to fly to avoid hitting anything. Bats use the same technique.

Kiwis find their food in the dark by following their noses. Unlike most birds, they have nostrils at the tip of their beaks rather than at the base. This gives them a very good sense of smell.

The only known nocturnal gull is the swallow-tailed gull from the Galapagos Islands. It has huge eyes for spotting prey at night.

Keeping track

Most birds have three or four toes, while some, such as ostriches, have only two. The way birds move on the ground often depends on their size. Small birds, such as sparrows, hop. Larger birds, such as geese, walk. Birds which spend most of their lives in the air, such as swifts, have such weak legs and tiny feet that they find walking or hopping almost impossible.

Keep a lookout for tracks in the damp mud on lake shores and riverbanks, or around any puddles that birds use as baths. Also look in the damp sand along seashores and in the snow. The shape and size of a bird's feet give several clues about its life. Finding bird tracks will help you to identify some of the birds living in a particular area.

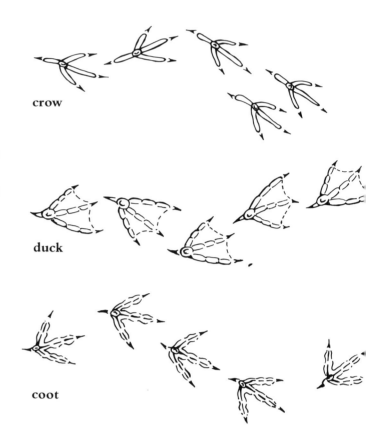

crow

duck

coot

pine siskin

toes

ankle

AMAZING FACTS

The African jacana, or lily-trotter, has the longest toes of any bird. They are up to 3 inches long. The jacana spreads its weight over its toes so that it can walk across waterlily leaves without sinking.

Parrots sometimes use their strong, curved beaks as extra feet to help them climb up trees.

Hoatzin chicks in South America are often born in trees that hang over water. If the chicks fall in, they have a special way of getting back up. They cannot fly, but have tiny claws on their wings for gripping the tree trunk so they can climb up again.

Eagles have such strong legs and feet that they can carry off prey almost as heavy as themselves. In 1932, a sea eagle even carried off a young girl in Norway.

Hold tight

Many birds roost, sleep, or rest perched on branches, yet they never fall off. When they land, the tendons in their legs tighten and automatically lock their toes shut around the branch. To release this grip, the bird has to contract (shorten) the muscles in its toes.

Sparrowhawk Birds of prey have long, curved talons for catching prey and tearing meat. Many have difficulty walking because of the talons.

Pigeon Like all perching birds, the pigeon's foot has three toes pointing forward and a single toe pointing backward for gripping branches tightly. All four toes are quite large. Pigeons walk "pigeon-toed," with the front of their feet turned inward.

Mute swan Like many water birds, the mute swan has webbed feet which help it to swim. The large feet have three toes in the web and a small hind toe. Swans also use their feet as brakes when they land on water.

Coot Coots and grebes have lobes of scaly skin growing between their toes. These act as paddles when they are swimming and stop them sinking into the mud on land.

Sandpiper Wading birds, such as sandpipers, have long legs for walking through deep water in search of food. Their weight is spread over long toes to stop them sinking into the sand.

Woodpecker Woodpeckers have long-clawed feet with two toes pointing forward and two pointing backward. These help the birds to grip on to tree trunks.

Making footprint casts

A good way of studying birds' tracks is to make plaster casts of any footprints you find. It is probably easiest to do this in your backyard, so that the equipment you need is handy. However, you can easily take what you need to the park and do it there.

Make a card collar from a strip of cardboard about 2.75 inches high. It should be large enough to fit around the footprints.

Put the collar around the prints. Place some plaster of Paris in an old jar and add water until you have a runny consistency. Carefully pour it into the collar so it reaches about halfway up.

Leave the plaster to set hard. Remove the collar and gently lift the cast up. Wash the cast in cold water.

Now you can try to identify which bird made the tracks. Use the clues given above and a field guide to help you.

Finding a mate

During the breeding season, competition among male birds to find a suitable mate is often fierce. Many have special ways of attracting a female. They sing and dance, show off their plumage, or bring gifts to impress her. Some birds mate for life. Others stay together for just one breeding season.

There are many things to look out for in the breeding season. Males and females of the same species sometimes look very different. The male is often much more colorful. Some birds grow brighter feathers for the summer breeding season. These then fade in winter. You can check all these details in a field guide. But don't get too close to breeding birds, and never disturb them.

Puffin Male puffins only have their brightly colored beaks during the summer breeding season. The blue, red, and yellow stripes help them to attract a mate. At the end of the summer, the outer layer of beak is shed and the puffins are left with a smaller, dull gray beak for the winter. Puffins are the only birds that molt their beaks.

Great-crested grebe The great-crested grebes of Britain perform a complicated courtship dance before mating. They face each other on the water and shake their heads. One bird dives, then rises straight up in the water. The other rushes away, then turns to face its mate. Both birds dive and reappear with weed in their beaks. They rise up, touch breasts, and shake their heads again.

Black grouse The male black grouse, also of Britain, has striking black, white, and red plumage whereas the female is dull brown. At breeding time, the males gather in communal sites, called leks. Each has its own small patch where it struts and scuttles, displaying its curled tail feathers, wings, and head tufts. Females fly in, choose a partner, and mate.

Mute swan The swans face each other, swaying their heads from side to side or dipping their heads in the water. They then extend their necks or bills vertically, before mating. Male swans perform victory dances after they have chased off a rival male. Pairs of mute swans mate for life.

Common tern Many male birds, including common terns, kingfishers, and bullfinches, give the females food as part of their courtship rituals. Once a common tern finds a mate, he presents her with a gift of fish. They also perform courtship dances.

Peacock You may see male peacocks in parks and gardens, fanning out their dazzling tail fans and shaking their feathers at the drab, brown females. They use the magnificence of their tails to attract the best females.

Singing skylark

Male songbirds, such as skylarks, use their voices to attract a mate, warn away rivals, and defend their breeding territories. Skylarks have a long, pleasing, liquid-sounding song. As they sing, they fly straight up into the air, hover for a while, then drop down to earth. The song flight may last for up to 10 minutes.

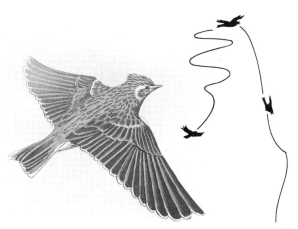

Making a nest

Most birds build nests to provide safe places to lay their eggs and raise their young. These nests come in a huge variety of shapes, sizes, and construction, and take varying amounts of time to build. They range from the cup-shaped nests of many woodland birds, to the gigantic platforms of branches built by golden eagles. Birds use a great variety of nest sites, too. Kingfishers nest in riverbank tunnels, pheasants in scrapes on the ground, and woodpeckers in holes in trees.

A small number of bird species don't make nests of their own at all. These include the cowbird which lays its eggs in other birds' nests and leaves them to be hatched and raised by the other birds. Some birds of prey, such as kestrels, take over old, abandoned nests.

WARNING! WARNING! WARNING!

It is illegal to disturb, or even photograph, nesting birds. **Never** steal eggs from the nest.

Cup shape The bird makes this shape by sitting in the center of the building material, turning its body and weaving the material into shape.

Lichen is placed on the outside to camouflage the nest.

Moss gives structure, insulation, and camouflage.

Feathers and hair provide insulation and warmth for the eggs and chicks.

Grass gives structure.

Cobwebs are used to anchor the nest to branches with their sticky strands. Cobwebs are also used to bind the nest materials together.

Nest materials

Birds may make thousands of trips to collect nesting materials. They tend to use natural materials which they find wherever they live. Some, however, will use anything. A crow's nest was once found, made completely out of eyeglass frames! These are some of the most common nest-building materials and their main functions:

Camouflage Lichen, pebbles, reeds.

Insulation Feathers, sheep's wool, animal fur, seedheads, horse hair, plastic bags, paper, mud, grass.

Structure Grass, plant stems, leaves, reeds, moss, twigs, mud, seaweed, barbed wire, string.

Swallow This bird builds saucer-shaped nests of mud, mixed with saliva. Nests are lined with dry grass and feathers. In spring, look out for swallows carrying mud in their mouths, as over a thousand mouthfuls of mud are needed to make one nest. Nests are built on ledges or under the eaves of buildings. Swallows return to the same site year after year.

Moorhen Typically, the moorhen makes a floating nest of reeds and water plants in the shallow water at the edges of lakes and reservoirs. It is often hidden among clumps of grass or reeds. The nest is raised to keep the eggs above water.

Heron The heron builds a platform nest of sticks, twigs, and reeds and usually lines it with grass. Herons often build their nests in large groups, called heronries, in trees above water. A heronry may contain hundreds of nests. Some herons nest in reed beds on the ground.

Cormorant Using seaweed, cormorants build mound-shaped nests on rocks and cliff ledges. Their nests are often part of a huge colony of nesting seabirds, which may include gannets, kittiwakes, puffins, and razorbills. Some species of cormorant nest in trees.

Looking at nests

In spring, look out for birds with their beaks full of nesting materials. Make a note of what items a particular species uses. How many trips do they make? Where are they building and how long does it take? Remember, always keep at a distance.

If you want to look more closely at a nest, wait for winter and the end of the breeding season. Many trees will have lost their leaves, making the nests easier to find. Note down the nest's shape, its location, what it is made of, and how different materials have been used. Has the bird used any unusual materials? Which bird did the nest belong to?

Eggs and chicks

All birds lay eggs, but the type and color of the egg depends on the species. Grouse and gulls, for example, lay their eggs on the ground. The color of the eggs camouflages them against their surroundings, protecting them from predators. Clutch sizes vary, too. Some birds, especially seabirds, lay just one egg. Others lay several times their own weight in eggs in one season.

The eggs need to be kept warm so that the chicks develop properly. This is the incubation period. Usually the female sits on the eggs, holding them against her brood patch, a bare patch on her breast. Gannets and cormorants do not have brood patches – they use their webbed feet instead! Some birds hatch in just 10 days. Other take over 60.

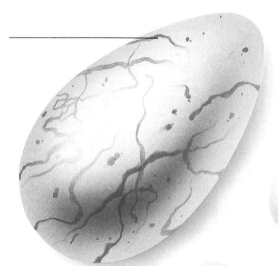

Murre A single egg is laid on a very narrow, bare cliff ledge. The pear shape reduces the chance of it falling off. Instead, it rolls in a circle and stays on the ledge. Different patterns may help parents to recognize their own eggs.

Woodpecker The woodpecker lays white, glossy eggs in holes in tree trunks. There is no need for the eggs to be camouflaged as they are well hidden inside the tree trunk. Woodpeckers, owls, and other birds that nest in tree holes all lay rounded eggs.

Magpie It builds a domed nest in tall trees. The 6-8 eggs are light blue or light green with dark markings. Despite being quite a bright color, the eggs are not noticeable from above because of the dappled appearance, which breaks up the outline of the eggs.

Kingfisher Kingfishers build their nests in burrows in the riverbank. They lay about 6-8 eggs. To keep the newly-hatched chicks well fed, the parents may have to catch over a hundred fish between them every day.

Semipalmated plover The plover lays its eggs on shingly seashores. The color of the eggs camouflages them among the pebbles. If a predator approaches, the parent bird distracts its attention by leaving the eggs and leading the predator away.

Grouse Eggs are laid in a scrape on the ground, lined with bits of plants. The brown blotches on the shells help to camouflage the eggs among bracken and heather.

Hatching out

It takes most chicks several hours to break out of their eggshells, although some of them only need 30-60 minutes. Eggshells are thin but very strong so chicks have a bony "egg tooth" on their beaks to chip their way through. This falls off shortly after they hatch.

Ducklings and goslings leave the nest almost immediately. Other chicks, such as songbird, pigeon, and woodpecker chicks, are blind, naked, and helpless. Their parents feed them constantly. Look out for the parents returning to the nest with their beaks full of worms, caterpillars, or other insects. How often do they feed the chicks? Some have to make hundreds of food-gathering trips a day. They feed the chicks as much as they can, so that they grow as quickly as possible and can leave the nest to fend for themselves.

AMAZING FACTS

The ostrich, the biggest bird in the world, also lays the biggest egg. It is equivalent to about 18 chicken's eggs. Its shell is strong enough to support a person's weight.

The albatross lays the largest egg of any seabird. It is also the heaviest, weighing up to 18 ounces. A royal albatross holds the record for incubating its eggs for 79 days before they hatched.

The bee hummingbird lays the smallest eggs. They are only slightly bigger than peas.

The blacksmith plover in Africa has to keep her eggs cool so that they do not overheat in the hot sun. She shades them with her outstretched wings.

Picking up the pieces

Look out for pieces of eggshell on the ground. Is there a nest nearby? Most birds carry the eggshell pieces away and drop them well away from the nest. They do this so as not to attract predators. For this reason, blackbird and starling eggshells are quite commonly found on lawns or in parks. If you see a nest lying on the ground, with egg shells scattered around, this may be the work of the bluejay who likes to eat the eggs and young of other birds.

More things to do

Sketching birds

Quick sketches of birds can make valuable records. Even if you can't identify the bird right away, you can compare your sketch to a field guide later on. Don't worry if your drawing is not a masterpiece. Rough sketches are also very useful for recording the important points about the bird you have seen. When you have finished your sketch, label any unusual features, particularly patches of color. Note down where and when you saw the bird, and how it was behaving.

Making a nest box

As more and more wild places are destroyed, birds have fewer natural sites to build their nests. A nest box in your backyard not only helps the birds but gives you an ideal opportunity to watch them.

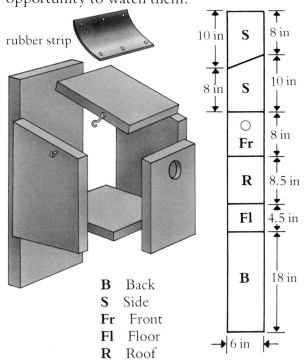

rubber strip

10 in	**S**	8 in
8 in	**S**	10 in
	○ **Fr**	8 in
	R	8.5 in
	Fl	4.5 in
	B	18 in
	6 in	

B Back
S Side
Fr Front
Fl Floor
R Roof

You will need: a plank of wood 6 in wide and 0.5 in thick; nails; rubber or leather strip.

1.   To make a basic, front-holed box, saw the plank of wood into pieces, as shown in the diagram.

2.   Nail or glue the pieces of wood together, as shown. Ask an adult to help you cut a round hole in the front with a drill or a saw. The hole should be about 1 in wide and should be about 5 in from the floor of the box, so that a cat cannot scoop the young birds out. Hinge the lid with a piece of leather or old rubber inner tube.

Tie the box firmly to a tree trunk with a length of wire. It should be about 10ft above the ground, out of the reach of predators, and out of direct sunlight and wind. This type of box should attract birds, such as nuthatches and tree sparrows. In the autumn, when you are sure the birds have left, clean out the box thoroughly in order to prevent the spread of disease.

Making a birdbath

Water is essential to birds for drinking and bathing. You can encourage birds to visit your backyard by making a birdbath. Do ask your parents for permission first, before digging the hole.

You will need: a trash can lid or plastic dishpan and some bricks.

1.   Dig a shallow hole in the ground away from bushes where cats may hide.

2.   Sink a trash can lid or plastic dishpan into the hole, or even support a lid on some bricks.

3.   Fill the bath with water and put a stone in the middle as a perch. Keep the bath full, especially in dry weather. Remember to break any ice that forms in winter but never put salt in the water to stop it freezing, or use hot water to break the ice. Both of these will harm the next bird to visit.

You can then observe the birds as they visit the water. Watch how most birds tip their heads back when they drink.

Building a bird feeder

Many birds die in winter when food is scarce and they cannot eat enough to keep warm. You can sprinkle food for the birds on the ground, but it is much better to make a simple bird feeder which you can support on a stake or hang from a tree branch. Only put out food for the birds during the autumn and winter months as there is plenty of food around at other times of the year. Also, some of the food you put out might harm young birds.

You will need: a piece of plywood, about 12×20 in; 4 strips of wood, 0.5 in high; wood preservative; a wooden stake 5-7ft long or nylon string (depending on the type of bird feeder); nails; 4 screw eyes; wood glue.

1. Glue the strips of wood to the top sides of the square piece of wood, leaving 2 in gaps on either side for water to drain away. Turn the table over and hammer two nails into each of the wooden side pieces to secure them. Coat the wood with wood preservative and leave it to dry.

2. To make a hanging bird feeder, now turn the feeder the right way up and put a screw eye into the corner of each side piece.

3. Cut four pieces of nylon string of equal length (approximately 20 in) and tie them to the screw-in eyes. Knot the other ends of the string in the center, or tie them in pairs so that you can hang the bird feeder across a horizontal branch.

4. If you are making a staked bird feeder, drive a sturdy wooden stake into the ground and coat with wood preservative. Take care not to place your bird feeder near to a tree or fence which a cat could use to leap onto the feeder. When it has dried, use two or four small metal angle brackets at the top of the stake to fix the bird feeder. If you like, add a couple of nails to the side of the bird feeder so that you can hang bags of nuts up in winter.

Feed the birds in the morning. Put some food under the feeder as some species of bird prefer to eat off the ground. The sort of food they will eat includes seeds and seed cakes (seeds pressed into cakes with oil), nuts (for example peanuts, not salted), fat scraps, and bread crumbs. Never give them salty foods. Keep a shallow dish topped up with water, so that the birds can drink as well.

Watch the birds feeding and notice whether they are shy or confident. Which ones are which?

Recognizing bird songs

Apart from courtship songs (see page 25), birds use many other calls to communicate with each other. Songs are also used for proclaiming territory or just to keep in touch with each other, and raise the alarm if necessary. These calls tend to be shorter and less musical.

As you gain in experience, you will be able to identify many birds by learning to recognize their voices. However, it is not easy so, if possible, start by going out with an expert who knows the calls already and can point them out to you. A good time to listen is at dawn or dusk when birds are at their noisiest.

Index

PRINTED IN BELGIUM BY

proost
INTERNATIONAL BOOK PRODUCTION